# The Life Raft

# the Life Raft

*Rise Above the Tides and
Rescue Your Dreams*

## CJ SCHEPERS

**Twinkle Prose Books**
**Santa Monica, California**

Copyright © 2014 by C.J. Schepers

*Cover and interior design by:* Jennifer Mola Design – **molaroad.com**
*Cover and interior photography:* **istockphoto.com**
*Author headshots:* Lexie Cole – **lexiecolephotography.com**

All rights reserved. No part of this book may be reproduced by any mechanical, photographic, or electronic process, or in the form of a phonographic recording; nor may it be stored in a retrieval system, transmitted, or otherwise be copied for public or private use—other than for "fair use" as brief quotations embodied in articles and reviews—without prior written permission of the publisher. For more information, contact CJ Schepers, Twinkle Prose Books, 1112 Montana Avenue, PO Box 868, Santa Monica, CA 90403, USA. Or visit cjschepers.com

Limit of Liability/Disclaimer: The publisher and author have done their absolute best to ensure accuracy of the contents this book; but hey, just like life, there are no warranties or absolutes here. The intent of this book is to offer inspiration that can help you in your quest of a better, fuller life.

**Library of Congress Control Number:** 2014915686
**ISBN:** 978-0-9915711-0-9
**Library of Congress Cataloging-in-Publication Data**
Schepers, C.J.
    The life raft : rise above the tides and rescue your dreams / CJ Schepers.
    p. cm.

1. Conduct of life –Quotations, maxims, etc. 2. Inspiration –Quotations, maxims, etc. 3. Motivation (Psychology) –Quotations, maxims, etc. 4. Mysticism – Quotations, maxims, etc. 5. Happiness –Quotations, maxims, etc. I. Title.
PN6084.H3 .S34 2014
152.42 –dc23

Printed in the United States of America

*This book is dedicated to everyone
I love and cherish, especially:
Ted and Emma, Valerie and Brooke.*

*Neither king's nor queen's
ransom would I trade for
the bounties of your love.*

# Introduction

## My Story

I'M FLOATING on a small wooden raft in the middle of the ocean, sun hanging low. My skin begins to prickle. Above me, I sense the bluest sky slipping into black. A flock of fears fly into my chest, heart pounding against ribs, a terrified animal trapped in its cage.

Suddenly, in the distance, a magnificent ship emerges from the thick brume. I plunge both arms into the freezing gray waters, rowing toward it like a chicken with my hair on fire. On cue, the waves swell higher. The wind blows harder. The air turns colder. And then, the boat turns away.

*Oh my god!* I scream. *Hey, I'm over here. Don't you see me?*

Instead, it only grows smaller and smaller, gliding back toward the horizon.

*I'm not going to make it . . . And I've come all this way.*

And then the ship—the one I thought would save me—is gone.

---

MY EYES OPENED. I was alive; lying in my dry, warm bed. But I knew what this nightmare had meant: my hopes, my dreams, my very life. They were all crumbling. Washing away. Tears gushed forth. OK, it was more like untethered wailing. I didn't want to freak out the neighbors, so I reached for a pillow to muffle the sobs. But then another part of me realized—this primal grief had released a heavy psychic pain. Truth be told, I'd been sinking for a long, long time.

*Anxiety embraced me. Sorrow squeezed my hand. Depression kissed my lips.*

In the beginning, these dark feelings had crossed my inner threshold as only temporary, tolerable houseguests. At some point along the way, however, they had settled in and made themselves at home. I had let them stay too damn long.

That is the moment I began to shift. I was fed up with feeling so wrung out and miserable. Like a frog stuck on the same stone and pondering its existence, my eyes blinked and opened wider. I could suddenly see farther out into the pond than ever before.

In search of answers that morning, I sat down to write out the major bumps and bruises of my past, then leaned back and took it all in. A heavy sigh shivered out of me. I guess I thought once I'd gotten all that crap out of my head and onto some paper, I'd feel better. But the facts only stared back at me. A dark swirl of sadness stirred in my gut.

Here I was, forty-something and college-educated—with a high enough IQ to match Einstein (at least when he was seven)! Yet, I was broke (and broken). Night after night, I'd flop in bed like a beached and dying mackerel wondering whether or not I'd survive. During the day, I guzzled caffeine and sucked down sugar to keep some semblance of functioning brain activity. As a freelance copywriter I often had to pound out ideas into wee hours of the night (believe me, those snappy headlines don't write themselves). Of course, none of this helped my unrelenting neck and arm pain. It had shadowed me for years. Decades. The pain varied in intensity: when it was low, it made me cranky; when it was high, it slammed me to the mat. Often stopped me from earning. More and more I found myself not able to make those credit card payments, urgent medical expenses, and basic life stuff like, uh, food and rent.

Yep, I was hanging by a thread all right. But I wasn't a quitter. Hey, if Nelson Mandela could endure thirty years in a crap-hole prison cell, I could survive the four walls of my small, dimly lit apartment; the stir of hunger; and the humiliation of driving a ramshackle car in LA—*um, couldn't I?* As a salt-of-the-Earth Midwest child, a modern-day tributary of English-Irish immigrants, I guess the one thing my DNA knew how to do was just "buck up" and keep slogging forward.

The following week I was reading the *Los Angeles Times* about a struggling, once-homeless actress, who regularly consulted with a modern-day witch. Soon after, she'd landed a huge movie role, her first Academy Award, and a major life upgrade. *Wow! I have to meet this miracle worker.* Now I admit: I've always believed (and still do) that powerful, positive forces exist in the world that we don't often see. A dreamer, a risk-taker, I booked half a dozen sessions with the motherly enchantress. After several months of burning "good-fortune" candles and soaking in bath oils of every kind she'd prescribed me, after doing everything the kind soothsayer said to, nothing had changed. Worse yet, I realized that I could've (should've) put the last several hundred dollars I'd blown with her on some badly needed massages for my neck and spine. This did nothing to boost my confidence or outlook on my future, to say the least. In fact, I could only feel that worse things were coming.

There's an old Taoist saying that, "When you're on the path you know it and when you're *not* on the path, you *don't* know it."

Well, I was lost as hell.

---

EVER SINCE I FIRST learned to read; words and stories had been my salvation, my teacher, my healer. My compass point on Earth. Words had gotten me through a childhood that nearly crushed me. I thought maybe they'd help me again. I'd once read about a study on aging that found the right words—at the right time— have the power to change your life. So I began to search intently and pan my surroundings looking for those pearls of wisdom that called to my heart and made sense to my soul. Little by little, I started feeding myself on pieces of courage, optimism, and pure determination from others (living or not). I remember the night I heard Amy Grant singing through the radio, "*It takes a little time sometimes ... To get your feet back on the ground ... It takes a little time sometimes ... To turn the Titanic around.*" Every word, every note, opened me up to something I'd eagerly cheered on for others, but denied for myself: the power of self-compassion.

After that, I feverishly researched and listened for the wise messages from others who'd survived life's hardships, too. Even though these words came from *outside* me, they were awakening something *inside*. They were the antidote to the poisoned apple I'd unwarily eaten. At some point, I started capturing my own thoughts, my own words. I'd like to say that a blue bolt of lightning shot out of the sky and into my spine. But it wasn't like that. There were moments, however, here and there, when the clouds began to part, and more and more reflections shimmered through, I could only guess, from within. Until one day, this passage revealed itself through me...

> *Be aware that too much remorse is like quicksand to the mind: the longer we flail about what we should have, could have, the deeper we sink. Let those feelings take their natural course, but don't let them take over your life!*

FOR THE FIRST TIME IN MY LIFE, I SAW THAT I OFTEN NEEDLESSLY PUNISHED MYSELF, AND REALIZED—NOTHING WOULD EVER CHANGE UNTIL I AGREED TO DROP MY OWN BLOODY WHIP.

And then, despite the fact I couldn't yet see dry land ahead, some part of me wrote...

> *Sometimes, when a dark storm blows in, and you're wondering how to keep your head above troubled waters, you've got no choice but to stay in the boat, hang on for dear life, and ride it out.*

SO IT WAS THAT I BEGAN TO FEEL A LITTLE BRAVER, LESS ALONE, AND MORE DETERMINED THAN EVER TO MAKE IT.

Then there was this truth that greeted me one day—followed by an even bigger truth...

> *I have failed at many things and that's a fact. But to say that I'm a failed human being because of my defeats is pointless; it means nothing. Even if I was nearly done with*

*this lifetime, such ebbs and flows are not who I am, nor are they the substance of my soul.*

IT WAS THEN THAT I REALIZED: IN LIFE, EACH OF US HAVE SWALLOWED BITTER PILLS. BUT IT'S A MISTAKE TO BELIEVE THAT WE <u>ARE</u> THE PILL.

It was like one hidden part of me kept reaching out to the rest. At first, it was this small, timid voice, a shy loner one ignores in a crowd. But once I'd felt it, and once I fully acknowledged its existence, it only grew louder, more confident. Then, gradually, I began to notice an inexplicable presence. Something I'd completely neglected...

*It was my Spirit—my <u>resilient</u> Spirit.*

It was sort of like Dorothy's "duh" moment in *The Wizard of Oz* when she realized that she'd held the power to get back home—all along. The secret solution had nothing to do with the hocus-pocus of those ruby-red slippers. Because believe me, I'd even tried *that*. No, the secret was in the journey because without it—she'd never have found the magic inside her. Some call it our essence, our soul, our energy—whatever; semantics don't matter. Like Dorothy who'd wandered so far, I'd been searching in all the wrong places for the key to release me from my shackles of fear and lack. I'd been hoping to stumble onto some kind of quick fix, instant-pudding cure. Something like, "Hey CJ, here are the five foreseeable stages of a life in distress and you've almost made it." Or, "These are the prosperity prayers brought to you today by your angels." Or, "Just do these three selfless deeds, and then glory be, you'll have it made!"

Except, life doesn't work that way, does it? We love to believe that we can totally control life . . . if we only knew its ultimate secret. It took me a long time to realize that our most magical qualities can never be found in superstitious practices, the belief systems of others, or one-dollar lotto tickets. No. I'm talking about the kind of magic that makes you realize, *Hey, I matter.* I was meant to live on this planet, in this body, at this particular time, for a reason. It's the kind of magic that defies the most harrowing odds, and retains its power even in the wake of the cruelest defeats.

---

I KEPT GOING BACK to that nightmare where I was lost in the storm of that deep, dark ocean. I obsessed about the massive ship that appeared and then quietly voyaged away from me. I kept thinking it must be a dead-on metaphor for my boatload of money, my one and only chance at a rescue, or my-ship's-finally-arrived success.

But then, in one moment, after writing and rewriting (and *rewriting*) this book you now hold, it dawned on me: the ship that had disappeared—well, that was ***me***. Like parents searching for their child lost in the fog, it was the words of others, and then my own, calling out to me to remember my strength. To remember who I am. These were more than words.

*They were the lifeline—back to myself.*

This book, *The Life Raft*, is as much about your hopes and dreams, as it is survival.

Its commitment goes beyond my story—and now flows into *yours*.

It's meant to remind each of us how to be courageous in the face of all uncertainty (and one's own history). To embrace the bold notion that life—despite setbacks, hardships, and tragedy—*can* get better. To help each of us rise above what are often (let's face it) unbearable circumstances.

Because as we each rise, we not only change our own story, but like ever-expanding waves, we change other lives, too.

And maybe, before we leave this body, we'll make our biggest splash yet!

Wherever you are in life, if it feels like a tidal wave has washed away your reservoirs of strength, then this is the very moment to look into the mirror and accept the call . . . to overcome.

Remember your power.

Pure Heart,

# How to Use This Book

LIFE. It's not a twenty-four clock. An eight-to five job. Or even a particular age. It's a series of moment-to-moment choices.

As your journey unfolds, allow *The Life Raft* to carry you through it—one day, perhaps one hour, one minute, at a time. It can be read anytime, day or night, as much as you like. Try reading these messages out loud. Soak up the images. See if you can *feel* everything on that one page with ALL of your senses. Use that moment, your moment, to absorb whatever's there for you. Then, make your own choices.

On each page you'll discover an inspiration from me followed by either: a) the wise words of another; or b) an Action Item, just look for the symbol ⊛. The Action Items occur now and then as a reminder, a gentle nudge for you to move in the direction you want. Actions can, and should, be taken often. Tough situations often pull us down into depression and numbness. We can feel paralyzed. We may abandon our abilities to take life into our own hands again. The antidote to this is not only self-discovery and self-compassion, but also *action*. Action helps us reclaim our inner strength and power, regardless of our situation.

This book was born to be your unconditional companion, guide, and Muse along the way . . . regardless of life's ever-changing circumstances. It's the way of the hero and heroine's journey—yours, mine, ours.

# The Promise to Persevere

All pain either shuts us down or wakes us up. You can hurt so much that you simply give up, crawl under a rock, and wait for some higher power to feel sorry for you. Or you can finally declare that this pain is an uncomfortable gift. You can find a way to catch up with your dreams, regardless.

"One must have the adventurous daring to accept oneself as a bundle of possibilities and undertake the most interesting game in the world—making the most of one's best."

–Harry Emerson Fosdick

# Lighten Up

Instead of lashing out at others or ourselves, we can turn the pain of feeling overwhelmed into moments of grace, humility, humor. We can see the truth in a non-dramatic light. Whether we've been careless, or someone has taken advantage of us, it's time to simply learn from the situation, and move on.

 Look at yourself as the main character of a well-told story. Write down one thing about your life that makes your heart laugh.

"Not everything that can be counted counts, and not everything that counts can be counted."

–Albert Einstein

# The Value of You

You can't slap a barcode on anyone's head and declare it the sum total of a life. Look at your child, your partner, yourself, and ask: How much is the soul truly worth?

"The world is full of abundance and opportunity, but far too many people come to the fountain of life with a sieve instead of a tank car . . . a teaspoon instead of a steam shovel. They expect little and as a result they get little."

–Ben Sweetland

# Go For It

Starting right now, if you could absolutely live your dream, what would you do? Hesitate? Walk away? Or leap for joy? The sooner we stop making excuses, the sooner we'll grab that dream by its rascally tail.

# Be Conscious

If you don't like the direction of your life, notice your wave of thoughts. Are they helping or hurting you? Thoughts affect our emotions, and emotions affect almost everything else—in and around us. Once you decide to make a critical shift in how you think and speak about your circumstances, life cannot help but respond in tandem.

"Hold a picture of yourself long and steadily enough in your mind's eye, and you will be drawn toward it."

–Napoleon Hill

# When Suffering Doesn't Work

When we fall short of a dream or goal, we often feel it's a mirror of our own self-worth, a harbinger of a long, bleak future. This heavy-clouded thinking only shuts us down. You've got to invest in, and love yourself through the drama. Because, baby, shining your light is the only way out.

"Someone helped me realize that I was in this financial crisis, regardless, and that suffering over it wasn't going to serve me. In fact, it was doing just the opposite—draining me of the strength I needed to slay my dragons in the first place."

–Kenny Golde, filmmaker,
author, *The Do-It-Yourself Bailout*

"I am the master of my fate. I am the captain of my soul."

–William Ernest Henley, "Invictus"

# Take the Wheel

We can't sit idly by and simply "wish" our ship to come in. We've got to breaststroke, crawl, or dog paddle our way there. We've got to keep our deepest promise to ourselves and do whatever it takes.

"Just trust yourself, then you will know how to live."

–Goethe

# The Secret to Being Brave

There will be moments when we find ourselves caught in a tempest, times when we lose our footing and slip, and days when we can't seem to find our way home. Accept this and keep on going.

"Life's challenges are not supposed to paralyze you, they're supposed to help you discover who you are."

–Bernice Johnson Reagon

# Answer the Call

Embrace challenges and use them to transform your life—into the one you were born to live. Whatever happens, allow it to serve up a magnificent opportunity to start moving in the right direction, at last.

# Nurture: You.

Generosity is a beautiful thing but some of us may give too much to others—at the expense of our own well-being. Except in times of dire circumstances, martyrdom and self-sacrifice can do more harm than good. What good are you to the rest of the world, if you dare not fill your own well?

"I have outgrown the need to suffer."

–Al-Anon Expression

# Believe. You Can. Do It.

When one has the courage to fail, one will eventually succeed. So believe in your talents. Believe in your abilities. Believe in your life.

"Most of our obstacles would melt away if, instead of cowering before them, we should make up our minds to walk boldly through them."

–Orison Swett Marden

"What lies behind us and what lies before us are tiny matters compared to what lies within us."

–Ralph Waldo Emerson

# Reach In, Rise Up

Whenever we're feeling anxious, we can light a candle and express a positive statement, asking for strength and guidance. This isn't about religion or avoidance. It's about opening a space in your mind to find new solutions—beyond what your ego thinks it already knows.

# Use Those Painful Feelings

Thorny emotions like anger, regret, and sadness serve a purpose. Instead of denying them, witness and then harness their energy as a catalyst for necessary change.

"Just like children, emotions heal when they are heard and validated."

–Jill Bolte Taylor
*My Stroke of Insight*

# Keep Going

There's fierce, quiet power in being Persistent. Keep going . . . trying . . . believing. Mentally sear "Persistency Pays" across your heart.

"Just don't give up trying to do what you really want to do. Where there is love and inspiration, I don't think you can go wrong."

–Ella Fitzgerald

"You can look the whole world over and never find anyone more deserving of love than yourself."

–Buddha

# Love Thyself

Today, take something for yourself: a massage to unwind the knots, a book to ignite the soul, or any delight that lifts your weary wings.

# Know That You Know

If you're feeling overwhelmed, seek advice, but not approval. Heed your own spark.

"Self-trust is the first secret of success."

–Ralph Waldo Emerson

# You're the Garden

Once you start planting, feeding, and nurturing the right kinds of seeds in your mind, you can't help but reap more of the good. Heck yes, it's simple. But are you doing it?

"Once in a while it really hits people that they don't have to experience the world in the way they have been told to."

–Alan Keightley

# Mission: Recover

Most days I cope. But some days I cannot. Whenever I'm feeling beaten to a pulp, I find it's best to put my troubles temporarily aside. Now and then, it's good to unplug the world, curl up with my heart, and regenerate.

---

"Escape is not a dirty word. None of us can face what's happening head-on all of the time."

–Sheldon Koop, American psychologist

# You're Learning

It takes strength to move through a tempest, and come out the other side. It takes courage to see the good in life, while facing the bad.

"I'm not afraid of storms, for I'm learning to sail my ship."

–Louisa May Alcott

"You don't drown by falling in the water; you drown by staying there."

–Edwin Louis Cole

# Be Bigger Than Your Story

We all have our stories, some rougher than others. But circumstances are circumstances; they are not <u>us</u>. Make a commitment to release (or revise) any sad story holding you back, keeping you stuck, or standing between you and your highest potential.

"The world is full of cactus, but we don't have to sit on it."

–Will Foley

# You Choose

Whenever I practice being neutral and almost Zen-like about my emotional triggers, it reminds me—the only one that can free me from the hook of my own anxiety—is <u>me</u>.

# Shed the Pain

Instead of getting caught up in the details of what should've, could've happened, what if we agree to reflect deeply on the pain—and then finally—release it?

"They say you should not suffer through the past. You should be able to wear it like a loose garment, take it off and let it drop."

–Eva Jessye

# Gentle Honesty

Try looking at your past, present, and future from a higher perspective. Notice what it is about your life choices that have brought you to this moment (good and bad).

"If you begin to understand what you are without trying to change it, then what you are undergoes a transformation."

–Jiddu Krishnamurti

"When walking through the 'valley of shadows,' remember, a shadow is cast by a light."

–H.K. Barclay

# Listen for the Light

I was miserably broke, in wicked pain, and earning far less than I needed to survive. I saw no proof that things would turn around. Still, something inside me kept whispering, *"Keep going, keep going, please keep going..."*

"For a long time it had seemed to me that life was about to begin—real life. But there was always some obstacle in the way, something to be gotten through first, some unfinished business, time still to be served, a debt to be paid. Then life would begin. At last, it dawned on me that these obstacles were my life."

–Alfred D. Souza

# Where's Your Focus?

Somewhere along the way, many people have forgotten that they are co-creators of their own world. To say there's nothing one can do about one's circumstances is b.s. illusion. Even if you shift the way you perceive something, you've already changed it.

"We must accept life for what it actually is—a challenge to our quality without which we should never know of what stuff we are made, or grow to our full stature."

–Ida R. Wylie

# Are You Willing to Grow?

Abundance is a feeling that desired possibilities are within your reach. I know it sounds kind of hippy-dippy—but if you're willing to grow—you can do almost anything.

"The greatest discovery of my generation is that human beings can alter their lives by altering their attitudes of mind."

–William James

# Catch More

We don't have to be happy about our challenges, but we can certainly choose to look for the good stuff, and practice feeling all of that. We can smile into the eyes of another, bubble up from a hug, and spot humor in the flaws.

"You are never given a dream without also being given the power to make it true. You may have to work for it, however."

–Richard Bach

# Step Up

I eventually learned that I had to quit making excuses for not giving attention to what made me feel most alive. Sure, you might not be able to quit your job and spend a year sailing the world. But you can take one sailing lesson. You imagine; then strategize; then act. That's how you get there.

# Courage Is Already Yours

Wherever you're at in life, no matter how dire things get, it's critical to believe in your ability to summon your best. Courage is the lucky coin you've forgotten you already own. Spend it well.

"Great occasions do not make heroes or cowards; they simply unveil them ... Silently and perceptibly, as we wake or sleep, we grow strong or weak; and at last some crisis shows what we have become."

–Brooke Foss Westcott

# Really Look

Every day, one must ask, "What exactly is in my control and what <u>isn't</u>?" It's so important to look at your entire picture with objectivity and self-compassion.

"Don't let what you cannot do interfere with what you can do."

–John Wooden

"Close scrutiny will show that most 'crisis situations' are opportunities to either advance, or stay where you are."

–Maxwell Maltz

# You're in Charge

Whatever it is you're facing, just "think" and "feel" it through. Make a plan. It's all about <u>your</u> next move.

"Being unready and ill-equipped is what you have to expect in life. It is the universal predicament . . . Circumstances are seldom right . . . You must always do with less than you need in a situation vastly different from what you would have chosen."

–Charlton Ogburn Jr.

# Perfect Is a Myth

People often say things like, "If I just had the time, I'd write that book" or "If I just had more money, I'd finally be happy". Truth is, we often create our own barriers by waiting for the perfect ingredients to magically appear (and, that just doesn't happen). Just relax and trust your inner guidance to help you hit the mark.

# Give Yourself a Break

Did you know that Albert Einstein got expelled from school and didn't read till he was seven? That Fred Astaire flunked his first screen test? Or that publishers rejected Jack London's earliest story six hundred times? The fact is everyone "fails." So give yourself a break!

---

"Start by doing what's necessary, then what's possible, and suddenly you are doing the impossible."

–St. Francis of Assisi

"For the personality, bankruptcy or failure may be a disaster. For the soul, it may be grist for its strangely joyful mill and a condition it has been secretly engineering for years."

–David Whyte, *The Heart Aroused*

# Accept the Challenge

If you're going through financial difficulties or <u>any</u> breed of intense challenge—then this is your moment to spread those invisible wings—and face the very thing you'd rather not.

"Celebrate what you want to see more of."

–Thomas J. Peters

## Joy Is Real

Remind yourself to taste, touch, hear, smell, and <u>feel</u> all the good stuff you've been taking for granted. Savor the toast and butter of life.

"If you don't like something, change it; if you can't change it, change the way you think about it!"

–Mary Engelbreit

# Why Thoughts Matter

No one on this planet lives a trouble-free reality. Yet, it's often the perception of our problems that make or break us. At first I didn't believe it. Until I began experimenting with consciously choosing my thoughts around a problem, and then I couldn't help but notice: I started experiencing more positive outcomes (including a stronger state of mind). This was huge; it changed the course of my life.

"If you believe that feeling bad or worrying long enough will change a past or future event, then you are residing on another planet with a different reality system."

–William James

# Get Real

Humans have this peculiar, self-defeating habit of prophesying negative outcomes for themselves. Yet, clinging to the pain and darkness never wards off more of the bad, does it? The sanest thing one can do is start making positive, rational thinking your new, ingrained norm.

"What's past is prologue, and the world awaits."

–Lisa Mantchev, *Eyes Like Stars*

# Sense Beyond

The mistakes are done.
The chalk dust has settled.
The future is a clear, clean slate.

# Recharge

For anyone dealing with a long bout of overwhelming obligations, at times it will be necessary to turn off the "smart" phone. Take a break and reclaim your life. No one can keep charging ahead—without a recharge.

"Don't take life too seriously. You'll never get out alive."

–Bugs Bunny

# You Are the Clay

Looking over my shoulder at my life so far, I see that every major struggle brought me closer to the person I was meant to be.

 We all have positive core qualities; e.g, being resilient, dutiful, disciplined, inventive, passionate, sensitive, etc. Write down your own and remember: call on them often to sculpt your own life.

# Be Unbeatable

Just when you think you cannot take one more step, somehow, somewhere, remember to inhale the source of your resilience.

"Trials teach us what we are; they dig up the soul, and let us see what we are made of."

–Charles Haddon Spurgeon

# You Are More

Instead of fretting and repeatedly analyzing why we experience less than we deserve, what if we dared to open ourselves, not only to the possibilities around us, but already inside us?

---

"You are more than you realize, more than you can define ... Your past is not your identity ... You, living now, is your identity."

–George Lawrence-Ell, *The Invisible Clock*

"Do what you feel in your heart to be right, for you'll be criticized anyway."

–Eleanor Roosevelt

# Point the Way

Many well-meaning people will have their own opinions on your circumstances. You can listen, of course, because they may very well have valuable insights. Yet, ultimately, always follow your deepest instincts, your own integrity compass(ion). That way you operate from the right place—for you.

"The past is finished ... Whatever it gave us in the experiences it brought us was something we had to know."

–Rebecca Beard

# Expect the Good

You've got to consciously look forward to all that's unlived and waiting to bloom. Whatever's happened in the past, keep expecting the good.

# The Legend of You

You are not the sum of your losses and gains. You, my dear, are the hero, the heroine of an epic adventure that's calling your name. So, how do you want your tale told?

"I was once afraid of people saying, 'Who does she think she is?' Now I have the courage to stand and say, 'This is who I am.'"

–Oprah Winfrey

"You willed yourself to where you are today, so will yourself out of it."

–Stephen Richards

# Think with Purpose

Positive thinking isn't fanciful thinking. It's about cleaning up the murky tide of our negative internal dialogue. Like regular bathing, we must habitually feed our subconscious minds something constructive and intentional, instead of being run by the bullroar of self-defeats.

"Each of us has a fire in our hearts for something. It's our goal in life to find it and to keep it lit."

–Mary Lou Retton

# Flutter and Fly

It's never too late to live out the pages of your life—
and make it an amazing one.

# Find a Way

Whatever our situation, we can't allow our dreams to fester or hide out in a drawer. We must find a way to share them, plan them, and if necessary, rework them till they sing. We must act to make our dreams a <u>fact</u>.

"Why not go out on a limb? That's where the fruit is."

–Will Rogers

# Release and Revise

Allow yourself some brief disappointment and upset, maybe a satisfying expletive, and even tears. Then figure out what the hell you can (or can't) do about it.

"If you can't solve a problem, manage it."

–Robert Schuller

"When one door closes another opens but all too often there is a long hallway in-between."

–Rick Jarow,
the anti-career guide

# Changing Course

For most of us, changing career paths takes longer than we first envisioned. Just keep your sights on the dream. It may not stick to the timeline you wanted, but it'll happen. Determents and setbacks are part of the journey.

# Get Going

When we talk about envisioning the life we want, it involves a lot more than sitting around, lighting a candle, and uttering an affirmation or two. There's another part equally vital and you don't want to miss it: it's taking action and doing whatever it takes to actually live it.

"The vision must be followed by the venture. It is not enough to stare up the steps. We must step up the stairs."

–Vance Hawner

# Illuminate

I finally woke up and realized—I had to take my disappointments and sorrows and turn them inside-out—so that one day they could become something beautiful, meaningful.

---

"You have a masterpiece inside you, you know. One unlike any that has ever been created, or ever will be…No one else can paint it. Only you."

–Gordon MacKenzie

# Reframe It

We can be angry for months, years, even a lifetime. Or we can feel this way for just one day, one hour, one minute. Speak your truth; then let it go.

"The problem is not that there are problems. The problem is expecting otherwise and thinking that having problems is a problem."

–Theodore Rubin

"Discontent is the first step in progress. No one knows what is in him (or her) till he tries, and many would never try if they were not forced to."

–Basil W. Maturin

# Dive Deep(er)

I'd never tell anyone to be happy with financial struggle. It's not a natural state of being. It leads to sickness of the body, mind, and soul. Find a way to rise above it, break through it, or dig a tunnel underneath it.

# Decide, Then Act

For two decades, all I did was hope for a better life, with very little action behind it. I had basically given up and was counting on a higher power to do all the work. Whatever our circumstances, we must keep turning to ourselves, keep putting forth the energy, while absolutely allowing in some form of divine assistance (often from places we'd never imagine) as part of the equation.

"Hope for a miracle. But don't depend on one."

–The *Talmud*

"Should you find yourself in a chronically leaking boat, energy devoted to changing vessels is likely to be more productive than energy devoted to patching leaks."

–Warren Buffett

# Know When to Change

There are those pivotal moments when we must bravely walk away from the old world that's draining us to clear space for the new.

"A lot of what we ascribe to luck is not luck at all. It's seizing the day and accepting responsibility for your future. It's seeing what other people don't and pursuing that vision."

–Howard Schultz,
Starbucks head honcho

# Heed Your Own Might

I went through some pretty desolate days when I simply turned to playing the lottery as my last chance at success. Trouble is, this kind of passive wishfulness gradually eclipses and undermines one's own awe-inspiring power.

# Hang Tough

Countless others have left a trail of missteps behind them before realizing their successes. If they're allowed to slip, stumble, and fall, then so are you!

---

 State out loud, "I did the best I could and now I'm rising above it by doing the following … " (absolutely fill in the blanks here—hey, don't ignore this—just do it!)

"Within us all there are wells of thought and dynamos of energy which are not suspected until emergencies arise."

–Thomas J. Watson Sr.

# It's an Inside-Out Job

I believe that before we are born, we excitedly and bravely choose the major struggles and challenges of our life so that we can draw forth more of our own greatness. But sometimes I do find myself wondering: *What the hell was I thinking? And why didn't someone "over there" try and talk me out of it!* (Well, perhaps the real me knew: I could handle it.)

"Great things are not something accidental, but must certainly be willed."

–Vincent van Gogh

# Use the Pain

Whether you desire more money, time, or meaningful work, start using this vexation of spirit to your advantage.

"The greatest thing is, at any moment, to be willing to give up who we are in order to become all that we can be."

–Max de Pree

# Be Stronger Than Your Ego

It takes true grit to seek counseling and advice, to let a friend help you out. I had the damndest time doing this because my pride wanted to be the One who always helped others (not the other way around). I now see: that was egotistical of me.

# Break Free

Try opening the windows of your mind to the bold, true concept that having more of anything (money, love, talent) doesn't mean others have less. It only means you have more to give the world.

"When patterns are broken, new worlds emerge."

–Juli Kupferberg

# Press On, Go Deeper

Any crisis—money, health, relationship—can be the greatest invitation to finally peel away your "mask." Vow to transcend the crisis (not ignore or succumb). Make it work <u>for you</u>, so it resonates with your own light.

---

"Life is not easy for any of us. But what of that? We must have perseverance and above all confidence in ourselves. We must believe that we are gifted for something and that this thing must be attained."

–Marie Curie

# Seize and Savor Life

Celebrate your survival! Life doesn't happen once things seem better. Life happens—as we live it.

---

"Birds sing after a storm; why shouldn't people feel as free to delight in whatever remains to them?"

–Rose Fitzgerald Kennedy

"If you are pained by external things, it is not they that disturb you, but your own judgment of them. And it is in your power to wipe out that judgment now."

–Marcus Aurelius

# Wake Up

When's the last time you looked up at the sky and saw nothing more than dark clouds?

# Why Not You?

Self-indulgent "woe-me" has never solved a single problem. Continually challenge yourself to be different, and grab your life by the balls.

---

"There is no chance, no destiny, no fate, that can hinder or control the firm resolve of a determined soul."

–Ella Wheeler Wilcox

# The Point of Having Faith

Faith isn't about being religious. Faith is, "I think incredible things can happen that I can't yet see." It requires us to step out and do what we must to take care of ourselves—while also braving the growth-giving trials that come our way.

"Give exceeding thanks for the mystery which remains a mystery still—the veil that hides you from the infinite, which makes it possible for you to believe in what you cannot see."

–Robert Nathan

# Get Your Grateful On

An energy of gratitude helps us become the kind of person others want to spend time with (including the time we spend with ourselves). Practice feeling appreciative for what you've got, while also allowing yourself to expect and want more.

---

"If you can't be thankful for what you receive, be thankful for what you escape."

–Voice Unknown

"It's not the load that breaks you down, it's the way you carry it."

–Lena Horne

# Be the One

You're not the only person to suffer on the ragged edge of injustice or get mugged by misfortune. Move in this world as the extraordinary soul that you are, one who acknowledges your inexplicable, formidable power and inspires others to do the same.

"Without heroes, we are all plain people, and don't know how far we can go."

–Bernard Malamud

# Find Your Allies

When facing barriers, call upon your cavalry of champions—those mentors, role models, even fictional characters that act with the very attributes you admire. They'll bolster you in your aim to reach higher and stretch the limits of what you once assumed was impossible.

 The past is BEHIND you, so leave it there. As boring as it may sound, it's important to take the smallest, finite thing that bothers you and just clean it up.

# Stop Stinkin' Up Your Thinkin'

Too much remorse is like quicksand to the mind: the longer we flail about what we should have, could have, the deeper we sink. Let those feelings take their natural course, but don't let them take over your life!

"You're going through the horror of it, you're going through the isolation of it, but you're being empowered by reminding yourself that you're connected to everybody else."

–Adam Arkin

# Feel Our Shared Strength

It's normal to feel vulnerable about the uncertainty of life. Just don't give in to the dark emotions: feel them, but don't give in.

# Mind Your Thoughts

Rebuilding your life calls for courage and brazen optimism. Even right now, if you can only fake your positive expectations, keep doing <u>that</u> till you begin to actually <u>know</u> it.

---

"Stand up to your obstacles and do something about them. You will find that they haven't half the strength you think they have."

–Norman Vincent Peale

"We are powerful, magical beings."

–Deepak Chopra

# Open Your Eyes

Why stay in a career that has you sleepwalking in a fabricated world of disenchantment, boredom, and negativity? Decide today to wake up to your own sense of wonder, vision, and inestimable value. You're a unique human being and spirit. So take a risk—move toward your passion and purpose—now.

# Cast Your Light

This is never a requirement, but more of a universal promise: if you've been through some tough times, you'll inevitably appreciate more of the good. Recognize how much you've survived and evolved. You're an example of what's truly possible—for all of us.

"We either make ourselves miserable, or we make ourselves strong. The amount of work is the same."

–Carlos Castenada

---

 Ignoring the problem doesn't work for me. I'm strong enough to take one kick-ass action toward healing my situation—now.

# Take Command

Which approach do you think gets us closer to living an amazing life—flailing and whining about an undesirable situation? Or, mapping out a strategy to change course?

"Keep away from people who try to belittle your ambitions. Small people always do that, but the really great make you feel that you, too, can become great."

–Mark Twain

# Hang with the Greats

A simple sigh, a gesture, even silence from a friend can so easily snuff out a fantastic dream. Realize that this subtle negative feedback has nothing to do with your vision or potential to make a richer life for yourself. It has more to do with the self-doubts of others.

"Instead of looking at life as a narrowing funnel, we can see it ever widening to choose the things we want to do, take the wisdom we've learned, and create something."

–Liz Carpenter

# Cleanse Your Heart

Absolutely give your heart the time it needs to grieve. Eventually, however, you must turn off the spigot of affliction, and start drinking from the fountain of intention.

# Invisible Change

It may take awhile for your life to get better, so expect to go up and down for some time; it isn't magically changing overnight—but rather transforming with every thought and action you take in the present.

"The difficult is what takes a little time; the impossible is what takes a little longer."

–Fridtjof Nansen

# Wise Up

Consider that without a chapter of challenges, your personal story might be deeply incomplete. These slices of life are what fuel your growth, make you real, and more fully formed.

"Adversity has the effect of eliciting talents, which in prosperous circumstances would have been dormant."

–Horace

"A stop sign is a gift for you to learn that moving in the same direction won't take you any place new."

–Rex Steven Sikes

# Take a New Path

You may feel like job loss, business failure, or a relationship breakup is the end of the road. But this is only a misperception of reality, one that's fleeting in the broad brushstroke of time.

# Flow with Power, Not Force

Getting anxious never produced any cures. No matter how much you find yourself shaking in your booties, slow down and breathe deeply to the quick of your being. Then make your next move with grace and determination.

"The only pressure I'm under is the pressure I've put on myself."

–Mark Messier

---

 No matter what's going on with my life, here's how I'll always be true to myself...

# Love All of You

Many of our so-called flaws or chips in the armor often have a positive purpose. Impatience can instigate necessary change. Stubbornness can evolve into measured resolve. And ultra-sensitivity often unlocks the gates of higher creative expression and healing—the kind that moves the entire world. So appreciate who you are, while fine-tuning all your lovely quirks and kinks. As long as you're serving the higher good, you can't go wrong.

"Most of the important things in the world have been accomplished by people who have kept on trying when there seemed to be no hope at all."

–Dale Carnegie

# Baby, You've Got This

Begin to expect great things from yourself, and successes will come. Maybe not instantly, but eventually, they will. You've just got to step up your belief in who and what you are.

# Live and Love Now

Putting off the joys of life only imposes a heavier tax on our psyches, and makes it that much harder to overcome challenges. Insist on delight, humor, and wonder. No matter what.

"Oh, the places you'll go, oh, the things you'll see."

–Dr. Seuss

"You are not here merely to make a living. You are here in order to enable the world to live more amply, with greater vision, with a finer spirit of hope and achievement. You are here to enrich the world, and you impoverish yourself if you forget the errand."

–Woodrow Wilson

# We Need You

Whenever you experience lack, pain, or heartache, try not to insulate yourself from others too long. Retreat when you must. But be plucky enough to reemerge and join a waiting world that needs you.

"I can be changed by what happens to me. But I refuse to be reduced by it."

–Maya Angelou

# Shift How You Relate

Whenever you feel yourself dropping into the habit of despair, remember: it's easier to commiserate about being broke (and broken) than to share those uplifting moments that can stir and embolden us all. Negative talk is the lame way out. Seek the smarter way in.

"There are times in everyone's life when something constructive is born out of adversity . . . when things seem so bad that you've got to grab your fate by the shoulders and shake it."

–James Champy & Nitin Nohria
on Lee Iacocca, *The Arc of Ambition*

# Fight for Life

If you feel like a tidal wave has washed away your reservoirs of strength, then this <u>is</u> the very moment to look into the mirror and accept the call to overcome.

"We learn the rope of life by untying its knots."

–Jean Toomer

# Consider, Then Do

Procrastination about pressing issues only clogs us with agitated thoughts and creates bigger waves in our psyches and, consequently, our lives. So choose now to take action regarding those concerns, one piece, one step, one lap, at a time.

"Our history is not our destiny."

–Alan Cohen

# Say Goodbye and Mean It

It's important to acknowledge and complete the past, so you can feel in charge of your life. This helps to build up your internal fortress of calm while releasing the residue of self-punishment. It frees you up to be more of who you really are.

# Bloom, Baby, Bloom!

Small, kind actions, even thoughts, can shift just one person's mood and then before you know it, another's and another's. If you want to make a difference out there, you've got to bloom, baby, bloom!

---

 This week, invest in some planetary goodwill. A smile to a stranger will raise your endorphins and lessen the loneliness for you both; a polite yield to a driver can open the space of grace and evaporate tension; a small, unexpected gift to a neighbor is a sign of your trust in humanity (and yourself).

# Be Open to Evolving

Intense challenges always reveal some part of ourselves that requires attention, perhaps calling on us to become more responsible and aware . . . nudging us to speak louder and assert our own worth . . . and mobilizing the inner moxie and talent we'd long suspected was there.

---

"Painful as it may be, a significant emotional event can be the catalyst for choosing a direction that serves us—and those around us—more effectively. Look for the learning."

–Louisa May Alcott

# See Past the Illusions of Doubt

Too much time is spent doubting our dreams; we have trouble seeing beyond what we "think" we already know. Even if you're heavily challenged right now (or, especially), imagine and truly feel what you want from life, without delay. Your visions <u>and</u> actions will move you closer to the real thing.

---

"Don't be afraid of the space between your dreams and reality. If you can dream it, you can make it."

–Belva Davis

# Pay Attention

There are many forces on Earth to help us create and live in spectacular ways. The sooner we can acknowledge our own best qualities, the faster we focus and expand.

"People deal too much with the negative, with what is wrong. Why not try and see positive things, to just touch those things and make them bloom?"

–Thich Nhat Hanh

"The great thing in the world is not so much where we stand, as in what direction we are moving."

–Oliver Wendell Holmes

# The Mountain Is You

I'm not perfect and neither are you. We were born to make mistakes and face rejection. Love more of who you are and reach deeply for your own magnificence.

# Leap into Your Life!

Only a handful of souls will have instant success and why that is, is not important. The rest of us need to look at our own full potential—with the intention to start moving toward it—right now.

---

 Forget comparing yourself to others. This is you, not someone else! So how do you want <u>your</u> full potential expressed? Write it! Declare it! Be it!

"Notice the difference between what happens when a man says to himself, 'I have failed three times' and what happens when he says, 'I am a failure.'"

–S.I. Hayakawa

# The Truth about Failure

I've failed at many things and that's a fact. But to say that I'm a failed human being because of my defeats is pointless; it means nothing. Even if I was nearly done with this lifetime, such ebbs and flows are not who I am, nor are they the substance of my soul.

# Claim Your Peace

Pushing your boat as fast and far as you can without ever stopping won't sustain you for the long-term. Now and then, you must claim the space to shut off your engine, and watch the sun, wind, and water dance.

"Reflection is one of the most underused yet powerful tools for success."

–Richard Carlson

# Own Your Happy

It's hypocritical to say money can't buy happiness, because in a way, it can. It can mean getting the healthcare you need...living in a cleaner, safer place...and spending more life energy on that which calls your name. The flip side of this, however, is never waiting for money to "make" you happy. Big mistake.

---

"Joy, has no cost."

–Marianne Williamson

"You can't stop the future. You can't rewind the past. The only way to learn the secret . . . is to press play."

–Jay Asher, *Thirteen Reasons Why*

# Shake Off the Muck

In times of misery, an ooze of shame can pull us down at the very moment we need to stand taller. Underneath this shame is a belief that we've done something wrong (or why else would we be in this situation)? But this is simply an illusion. None of us knows what's best without the favors of experience and hindsight.

# Kick It Up

There are slices of one's life when great expectations don't materialize and anticipation melts into despair. Maybe that kind of response is humanly unavoidable, but we must be careful not to wrap ourselves in blankets of it. We've got to keep pouring fresh, fervent hopes and plans into our psyche. It's the only way to kick up our legs and start running through the tall green grass, again.

---

"There is some good in this world, and it's worth fighting for."

–J.R.R. Tolkien, *The Two Towers*

"You are not broken. You are not a problem to be solved. Solving your 'problem,' whatever you perceive your problem or problems to be, is not the key to happiness."

–Golda Poretsky

# You Are Not Broken

Insecurity is the same vibration whether it's about a relationship, money, or self-image. It's a belief that if you don't win the approval of others, you'll end up in an unloved place. Recognize it as only a feeling and not the substance of <u>you</u>.

"What ought one to say then as each hardship comes? I was practicing for this. I was training for this."

–Epictetus

# More Prepared Than You Think

Whatever tragedies and traumas you've met with, even worse events could have crossed your path. Never deny the reality of your pain, yet be aware that these sorrows also contain an unknown gift that may not reveal itself for some time.

# Hold Yourself Closer

Wading through the deepest end of our woes, we may be tempted to punish ourselves. To truly move onward and upward means giving up the ghost of guilt, the specter of shame and regret. Cut loose any remains of contempt—and hold yourself closer.

---

"Love yourself first and everything else falls into line. You really have to love yourself to get anything done in this world."

–Lucille Ball

# Dispelling the Inkiness

Inky corners of your mind may pull at you to simply give up; however, a lot of souls in this Universe are rooting for you to make it. Allow moments of forgiveness, grit, and mercy to lead you when you're hurting most.

―――

"There will be something, anguish or elation, that is peculiar to this day alone. I rise from sleep and say: Hail to the morning! Come down to me, my beautiful unknown."

–Jessica Powers

"When I let go of what I am, I become what I might be. When I let go of what I have, I receive what I need."

–Tao Te Ching

# How to Handle Crap from Your Past

The plan was to hold onto the sufferings of my past, and that way, the Universe wouldn't dare throw further pain my way. Of course, this strategy didn't work. It's like traipsing through manure, then leaving shit on your shoes to avoid stepping on any more crap. Whenever a negative wave hits you, feel the wound. Then, observe it from a distance. While you may never fully release it, you do, however, get to choose whether you're going to permit it to stink up the rest of your life.

# Who's Got Your Back?

Like all things that fall out of balance, there's always a tipping point—a time to be the saner voice that says, "enough is enough." This includes paying closer attention to the actions of your leaders, gurus, and politicians. Ask yourself: who's <u>really</u> got your back? Listen for the truth; demand all the facts. Don't settle for meaningless sound bites (or they may take a bite out of you!).

---

"Strength is taking charge of your own destiny and not waiting on others to do so. You don't have to swear and drink and beat people up and slay monsters...But when decisions have to be made, a strong character makes them and doesn't wait for someone else."

–Mur Lafferty

# Flat-Out Full-Strength

Any crisis can make us feel terribly vulnerable and scared, at which point, we tend to pull back on our real voice, to hide who we are, or what we could be. But that's precisely the place to express your truest self—at flat-out full-strength.

---

"Never be bullied into silence. Never allow yourself to be made a victim. Accept no one's definition of your life, but define yourself."

–Harvey Fierstein

# Rescue Your Dreams

Invest in you and what you can offer the world, not as a means to an end, but as a day-to-day journey toward something great. It's time to rise above the tides and rescue your dreams.

---

"No star is ever lost we once have seen, we always may be what we might have been."

–Adelaide Anne Procter, "A Legend of Provence"

# Ocean of Support

Despite what our egos like to think, no man or woman is an island. To everyone here, you were my biggest ocean of support when I needed it most. I never could've navigated all those uncertain waters and find safe harbor for this book without you!

Pure (Grateful) Heart,

Arsi Armaghanian
Haig Armaghanian
Pam Bard
Philomena Benz-Howell
Anna Bogdanovich
Marie Bretz
Robert Bretz
Deborah Brooks
Tisha Bryant
Minda Burr
Sandra Cary
Toni Christensen
Adolpha Cole
Nyk Cole
Lori Cooper
Craig Copeland
Catherine Curry-Williams
Annie Devarennes
Dave Edwards
Valerie Edwards

Shirin Esfahani
Elena Yates Eulo
Terry Formanek
Mary Gavlik
Todd Gewant
Marilyn Kentz
Jason Klassi
Suze Lanier-Bramlett
Ignacio Lopez
Lee Lucas
Samantha Harper Macy
Jeff MacCorkle
Brooke Maile
Jon Maile
Megan McLane
Jan Merrill
Bardia Mesbah
Jennifer Mola
Tony Newell
Kim Olsen

Cathey Painter
Gene Pascucci
Lisa Pascucci
Lucinda Piligian
Shannon Presby
Nancy Rosas
Janice Ryan
Brooke Schleiger
Peter Snell
Wanda Snell
Sue Springman
Tony Springman
Pat Tallman
Jim Ward
Johanna Whetstone
Patricia Whetstone
Rob Whetstone
Ted Whetstone
Jenny R. Williamson
Clara York Presby

## About the Author

Lexie Cole Photography

A ***bona-fide life crisis survivor***, CJ Schepers is a professional ghostwriter, book editor, and former religion reporter. Through her journey, she's experienced many of life's biggest lumps in one long, relentless stretch, including a violent childhood and her mother's death at fifteen; teen pregnancy, divorce, and single parenthood; debilitating chronic pain and disability; unemployment, financial failure, and more. All of this led her into deep waters of depression and despair. Ultimately, it was the words of others, and then her own, that became the literal lifeline—back to herself. CJ's purpose is to give us hope. Hope in our darkest moments, and our loneliest, most terrifying junctures.

She has two groovy daughters and three spunky g-kids, and lives in Santa Monica with her partner Ted and their crazy, adorable cats. CJ's current passion is ***Blackcat-Whitecat: The Interdimensional Tails***, a sci-fi fantasy book series that she's co-writing with her very first cat Emma (who currently resides on "the other side").

www.ingramcontent.com/pod-product-compliance
Lightning Source LLC
Chambersburg PA
CBHW051941290426
44110CB00015B/2061